Grammar
in practice 2

40 units of
self-study
grammar
exercises

Roger Gower

with tests

CAMBRIDGE
UNIVERSITY PRESS

CAMBRIDGE UNIVERSITY PRESS
Cambridge, New York, Melbourne, Madrid, Cape Town, Singapore, São Paulo

Cambridge University Press
The Edinburgh Building, Cambridge CB2 2RU, UK

www.cambridge.org
Information on this title: www.cambridge.org/9780521665667

First published 2002
3rd printing 2005

Printed in Italy by Legoprint S.p.A.

A catalogue record for this publication is available from the British Library

ISBN-13 978-0-521-66566-7
ISBN-10 0-521-66566-3

Contents

1 She's an accountant

be (present simple)

Positive		Short form	Negative		Short form
I	am	I'm	I	am not	I'm not
he/she/it	is	he's	he/she/it	is not	isn't / 's not
we/you/they	are	we're	we/you/they	are not	aren't / 're not

Question			Answer					
Am	I			I	am.		I'm not.	
Is	he/she/it	happy?	Yes,	he/she/it	is.	No,	he/she/it	isn't.
Are	we/they			we/they	are.		we/they	aren't.

A Write short answers.

> *Ms Yukie Yoshida*
>
> SALES MANAGER
> KBS Broadcasting Corporation
>
> http://www.kbs.co.ip

> Ms Judith Frey
>
> **COMPUTER ENGINEER**
> Euromett •GERMANY
>
> http://www.euromett.de

> Mr Majid Al Zahrani
>
> ACCOUNTANT
> MPND Bank
> Riyadh   Kingdom of Saudi Arabia

> **Mr Andre Melo**
>
> **Advertising Manager**
>
> Advanta Alimentos
> São Paulo Brazil

1 Is Euromett's web page www.euromett.de?   *Yes, it is.*

2 Is Advanta Alimentos a Japanese company?   ....

3 Is Majid Al Zahrani from Saudi Arabia?   ....

4 Are Yukie Yoshida and Andre Melo managers?   ....

5 Is Andre Melo from Germany?   ....

6 Are Yukie Yoshida and Judith Frey teachers?   ....

B Write questions and answers.

1 Yukie Yoshida/a sales manager?

Is Yukie Yoshida a sales manager?   *Yes, she is.*

2 Euromett/a Polish company?

3 Advanta's offices/in São Paulo?

4 Mr Al Zahrani/an accountant?

5 KBS's web page/www.yukie.com?

6 Mr Melo and Mr Al Zahrani/from Germany?

C Complete the sentences with the positive form of *be*.

1 My name *'s* Majid.

2 I _____ from Saudi Arabia. I _____ an accountant.

3 This _____ Andre. He _____ from Brazil.

4 Their names _____ Judith and Yukie.

5 We _____ interested in politics.

6 She _____ the sales manager of a big company.

7 It _____ very hot in here.

D Complete the sentences with the negative form of *be*.

1 They *aren't* Hungarian. They're German.

2 She _____ interested in computers.

3 I _____ a computer engineer. I'm an accountant.

4 We _____ from Tokyo. We're from Osaka.

5 Judith Frey _____ Brazilian.

6 Majid Al Zahrani _____ a sales manager.

E Complete the sentences about you.

1 I *'m 20* years old.   4 I _____ Scottish. I _____.

2 I _____ years old.   5 I _____ a company manager.

3 My name _____.   6 I _____ interested in _____.

2 Has he got a passport?

have got

Positive				Negative			
I/We/You/They	have got /'ve got	a coat.		I/We/You/They	have not got /haven't got	a coat.	
He/She/It	has got /'s got			He/She/It	has not got /hasn't got		
Question				**Answer**			
Have	I/we/ you/they	got your book?	Yes,	I/we/ you/they	have.	No,	I/we/ you/they	haven't.
Has	he/she/it			he/she/it	has.		he/she/it	hasn't.

A Complete the sentences about the man and the woman with *have got*.

1 ...._The woman's got_........ dark hair.
2 .... a moustache.
3 .... small ears.
4 .... a long nose.
5 .... short hair.
6 They .... glasses.

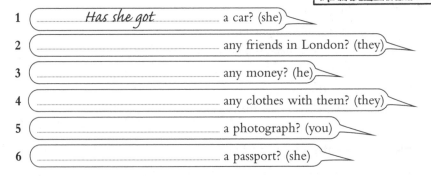

B Complete the questions.

1 (........_Has she got_........ a car? (she)
2 (.... any friends in London? (they)
3 (.... any money? (he)
4 (.... any clothes with them? (they)
5 (.... a photograph? (you)
6 (.... a passport? (she)

C Write questions and short answers.

1 (UK/a president? ..... *Has the UK got a president?*)
   No, it hasn't.

2 (the USA/a president? .....)

3 (Japan/blue flag? .....)

4 (Russia and the USA/a king? .....)

5 (the USA and India/a president? .....)

6 (Japan/a red and white flag? .....)

D Complete the sentences with *have got*.

1 The UK ..... *has got* ..... a queen.
2 The USA ..... a king or queen.
3 India ..... a president.
4 The UK and Sweden ..... a president.
5 Japan ..... a red and white flag.
6 The USA and the UK ..... red, white and blue flags.

E Complete the sentences about you and your country.

1 My country ..... a queen.
2 My country ..... a president.
3 My country ..... a king.
4 I ..... a US passport.
5 I ..... friends in London.

3 That's a good idea

	this/these	*that/those*
Singular	**This** coat is lovely.	**That** dress is nice. **That**'s a nice dress.
Plural	**These** gloves are cheap.	**Those** shoes are expensive.

this year/**this** month/**this** Tuesday; call **this** number: 258258

Responding: 'Sorry.' **'That**'s OK.'   'Let's go.' **'That**'s a good idea.'

On the phone: Hello. Is **that** Jo? (=Are you Jo?) **This** is Dan. (=I'm Dan.)

A Complete the adverts with *this*, *that* or *these*.

1. **COMPUTER WORLD.** Open ___*this*___ Sunday from 9 am.

2. **Buy** _____ perfumes and get another one free!

3. **EDINA FASHIONS:** Sale on _____ month.

4. **JETSET TRAVEL:** Two nights in Rome from only £50? _____'s right.

5. Phone _____ number now: 020 8143 2616.

6. **TVs, videos, CD players:** you can find all _____ things at Ace Electrical shops – and lots more!

B Complete this phone conversation with *this*, *that*, *these* or *those*.

Jo: Hello?

Martin: Hello, is (1) ___*that*___ Jo?

J: Yes, it is.

M: Hi Jo, (2) _____ is Martin. Jo – have you got a phone number for (3) _____ people in Singapore?

J: Hold on … I think (4) _____ is it: 651721186.

M: Thanks.

J: (5) _____'s OK.

M: Sorry? I can't hear you. (6) _____ mobile phones are terrible.

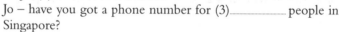

4 Is there a café?

Positive	Negative	Question	Short answer
There's a restaurant.	**There isn't** a gym.	**Is there** a café?	Yes, **there is.** No, **there isn't.**
There are some shops.	**There aren't** any offices.	Are **there any** car parks?	Yes, **there are.** No, **there aren't.**

A Complete this job advert with *there is* or *there are*.

Work for KMT Consulting:

(1) *There are* a lot of exciting new jobs at our head office in London.

(2)＿＿＿＿ over 1000 people at our London office and

(3)＿＿＿＿ six company offices worldwide.

At KMT:

(4)＿＿＿＿ an excellent company restaurant.

(5)＿＿＿＿ a modern gym.

(6)＿＿＿＿ a great company shop.

Send your CV to Amy Mason.

B Look at this plan of the London office of KMT Consulting. Write questions and answers.

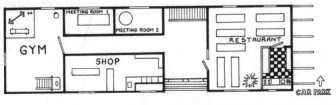

1 shop? (*Is there a shop?*) *Yes, there is.*

2 two restaurants? ( ) ( )

3 a café? ( ) ( )

4 car park? ( ) ( )

5 meeting rooms? ( ) ( )

6 gym? ( ) ( )

5 Be careful!

Imperatives

Positive	Negative
Go. Turn left.	Don't go. Don't turn left.

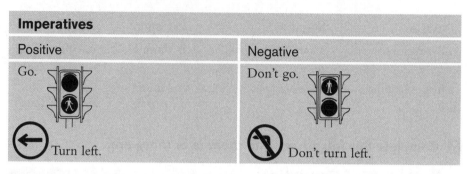

A **Write an imperative for each sign. Use the verbs in the box.**

~~smoke~~   eat this   be careful   drink the water   turn left   stop

1 _____*Don't smoke.*_____
2 _____
3 _____
4 _____
5 _____
6 _____

B **Look at the map and complete the directions to the museum. Use the verbs in the box.**

cross   take   walk   turn   ~~turn~~
turn   ~~come~~   go   pass   cross

HOTEL
THAMES STREET
CAR PARK
MUSEUM
STATION

(1) _____*Come*_____ out of the station and (2) _____*turn*_____ right. (3)_____ along the road and (4) _____ left. (5) _____ straight on and (6) _____ the bridge. (7)_____ the hotel on the right. (8) _____ the second turning on the left. At the car park (9) _____ right and (10) _____ the road.

6 It's her phone

Possessive adjective			Possessive pronoun		
This is	my your his her its our their	car.	This car is This is	mine. yours. his. hers. ours. theirs.	**Whose** is this? It's **mine.** ! it's = it is its = possessive Paris is famous for **its** cafés. **It's** a great city. ! a boy and **his** sister (**not** a boy and **her** sister)

A **Follow the lines. Then complete the sentences with a possessive pronoun or adjective.**

1 It's ___their___ newspaper.

2 It's _____ book.

3 The football is _____ .

4 The mobile phone is _____ .

5 The bags are _____ .

6 They're _____ football boots.

7 They're _____ sunglasses.

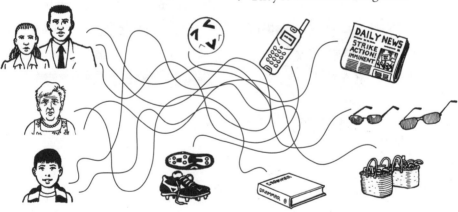

B **Complete the sentences with a possessive pronoun or adjective.**

1 It isn't his newspaper. It's ___ours___ . (we)

2 They're _____ sunglasses. (we)

3 It's _____ football. (I)

4 They aren't your bags. They're _____ . (I)

5 It isn't his mobile phone. It's _____ . (we)

6 They aren't my football boots. Are they _____ ? (you)

7 Are they _____ sunglasses? They aren't mine. (you)

7 I can read English well

		can	verb	adverb
Positive	I/He/She/It/We/You/They	can	speak English	**very well.** **quite well.**
Negative	I/He/She/It/We/You/They	can't	speak English	**very well.** **at all.**

Question			Answer		
Can	I/he/she/it/we/you/they	speak English?	Yes,	I/he/she/it/we/you/they	can.
			No,		can't.

ⓘ She can speak English. (**not** ~~She can to speak English~~)

A Look at the information about students on a languages course. Complete the sentences.

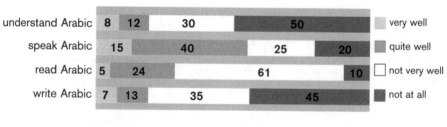

understand Arabic	8	12	30	50	▨ very well
speak Arabic	15	40	25	20	▨ quite well
read Arabic	5	24	61	10	☐ not very well
write Arabic	7	13	35	45	▧ not at all

1 45 students *can't write Arabic at all.*

2 61 students ....

3 15 students ....

4 8 students ....

5 13 students ....

6 10 students ....

B Write questions with *can*.

1 (write/Chinese?) *Can you write Chinese?*

2 (read/Russian?) ....

3 (speak/Japanese?) ....

4 (understand/English?) ....

5 (speak/Spanish?) ....

6 (understand/Arabic?) ....

8 My friend's house

Singular (+ 's)

my sister**'s** car; Jon and Sarah**'s** car; This car is my sister**'s**.

today**'s** newspaper; a week**'s** holiday
I'm at Jon**'s**. (=Jon**'s** house) the newsagent**'s** (=newsagent**'s** shop)

Plural: regular (+ s')	Plural: irregular (+ 's)
my parents**'** car; my two friends**'** house	the children**'s** room; the men**'s** changing room

ⓘ *We use 's/s' for people/time expressions.*
*We use **of** for things/places: the end **of** the street; the capital **of** Poland.*
*We say: house keys (**not** ~~the house's keys~~); car door (**not** ~~the car's door~~).*

A Put an apostrophe (') in the correct place.

1 his father's house
2 Pauls car
3 womens hair
4 Tom and Pat Smiths car
5 your parents names
6 yesterdays newspaper
7 my bosss desk
8 the babies toys
9 a nurses job

B Underline the correct form.

1 The engine is in **the back of the car** / **the car's back**.
2 These are **the prices of today** / **today's prices**.
3 What's **the car's make** / **the make of the car**?
4 Have you got **the driving licence of your wife** / **your wife's driving licence**?
5 There's a garage on **the street's corner** / **the corner of the street**.
6 Here are the **car's keys** / **car keys**.
7 The spare wheel is in **the front of the car** / **the car's front**.

CAR HIRE

C Look at the words in brackets. Then make sentences about you.

1 My *father's first name* is *Antonio.* (father/first name)
2 My_____ is _____ (mother/first name)
3 My_____ is _____ (mother/favourite food)
4 My_____ is _____ (best friend/favourite sport)
5 My_____ is _____ (country/most famous writer)
6 My_____ is _____ (doctor/name)

9 Some good advice

Countable nouns		Uncountable nouns
Singular	Plural	(+ singular verb)
There's **a car** outside.	There **are two cars** outside.	There's **luggage** in the car.
some/any		
Positive	There's **a** suitcase. (singular) There **are some** suitcases. (plural)	There's **some** luggage.
Negative	There **aren't any** suitcases.	There **isn't any** luggage.
Countable		Uncountable
dollar(s), coin(s) suggestion(s) job(s) detail(s) suitcase(s) minute(s), day(s)		money advice work information, news luggage time

ⓘ *We can use **a piece of** with many uncountable nouns*: a piece of advice/information.

A Circle the correct word(s).

1 Find **a job** / **a work** at www.jobs100.com

2 For more **information** / **informations** go to www.findout123.co.uk

3 Go to www.travelnow.co.fr for hundreds of **advice** / **suggestions** for your summer holidays.

4 For free **advice** / **suggestion** about the law go to www.youandthelaw.org

5 Find **work** / **job** in America with www.xyz33.com

6 You can win thousands of **dollars** / **money** at www.cashdell.com

B Complete the sentences. Use *a, some, any* or *piece of*.

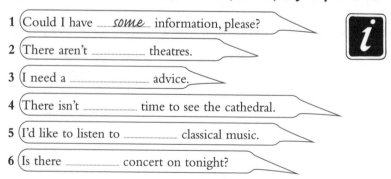

1 Could I have ____*some*____ information, please?

2 There aren't _____ theatres.

3 I need a _____ advice.

4 There isn't _____ time to see the cathedral.

5 I'd like to listen to _____ classical music.

6 Is there _____ concert on tonight?

10 I know you

Subject pronouns	Object pronouns	Verb	(+ preposition)	object
I	me	Come	with	me.
you	you	Look	at	him.
he	him	Phone		me.
she	her			
it	it			
we	us			
they	them			

A Circle the correct pronoun.

1 Look at **she** / **her**.

2 Help **me** / **I**.

3 My brother likes **they** / **them**.

4 Listen to **he** / **him**.

5 Phone **she** / **her**!

6 Can **he** / **him** drive?

7 Yes, **they** / **them** have.

8 Write to **us** / **we**.

B Write sentences with the words in the correct order.

1 $300 / me / bring   *Bring me $300.*

2 bag / in / it / put / the

3 you / tomorrow / telephone / we'll

4 soon / see / you'll / them

5 speak / her / to / don't

6 leave / your / me / car

7 them / come / with / don't

15

C Read about the play *Romeo and Juliet* and complete the answers to the questions. Use pronouns.

Romeo and Juliet
by William Shakespeare

Juliet Capulet and Romeo Montague live in Verona. Romeo loves Juliet but his family, the Montagues, hate Juliet's family and the Capulets hate Romeo's family. Juliet's parents want her to marry Count Paris but Juliet hates Paris and loves Romeo. Romeo kills Juliet's cousin, Tybalt, in a fight. At the end of the play Romeo and Juliet die – Romeo drinks poison.

1 How do the Montagues feel about the Capulets? _They_ hate _them_.
2 How does Romeo feel about Juliet? _____ loves _____.
3 How do the Capulets feel about the Montagues? _____ hate _____.
4 How does Juliet feel about Romeo? _____ loves _____.
5 How does Juliet feel about Paris? _____ hates _____.
6 What does Romeo do to Tybalt? _____ kills _____.
7 What does Romeo do with the poison? _____ drinks _____.

D Answer the questions for you.

1 What do you think of English grammar? _I love it._
2 What do you think of football? _____
3 What do you think of TV quiz shows? _____
4 What do you think of your country's leader? _____
5 What do you think of your manager/best friend? _____
6 What does your manager/best friend think of you? _____

Test 1 (Units 1-10)

A Circle the correct form.

1 **Have / Has** you got any children?
2 **This / These** shoes are expensive.
3 **Is there / Are there** a gym?
4 How many people **there are / are there**?
5 Is this **your / yours**?
6 What's **it's / its** name?
7 She can cook very **good / well**.
8 **Is there / Are there** any information?

$\boxed{8}$

B Complete the sentences with *be* in the correct form.

1 _____ you from Argentina?
2 This _____ Mandy.
3 _____ Jane and Bill English?
4 No, they _____ .
5 _____ I late?
6 No, you _____ .

$\boxed{6}$

C Write sentences with *have got* in the correct form.

1 I/not/any sisters. _____
2 Russia/a president? _____
3 The USA/not/a king. _____
4 we/not/any money. _____
5 they/the tickets? _____

$\boxed{5}$

D Complete the sentences with a positive or negative imperative. Use the verbs in the box.

| be drive drive stop stop |

1 _____ on the left in the UK.
2 _____ careful in bad weather.
3 _____ at red traffic lights.
4 _____ on a motorway.
5 _____ on the left in the USA.

$\boxed{5}$

E Complete the sentences with an adjective or pronoun.

1 They're _____ . keys (we)

2 He likes _____ . (I)

3 Those books are _____ . (I)

4 Listen to _____ . (we)

5 This pen is _____ . (you)

6 That's _____ bag. (he)

6

F Write the words with the possessive ('s, s' or of).

1 (my parents/house) _____

2 (my mother/coat) _____

3 (Germany/the capital) _____

4 (today/newspaper) _____

5 (the children/room) _____

5

G Complete the sentences with can or can't.

1 Sorry, I _____ English at all. (speak)

2 _____ you _____ music? (read)

3 He _____ Spanish quite well. (understand)

4 _____ you _____ Arabic? (write)

5 Sorry, I _____ you very well. (hear)

5

H Complete the sentences with a, some or any.

1 We haven't got _____ money.

2 There's _____ luggage in the car.

3 I'd like _____ piece of advice.

4 I've got _____ work to do.

5 Have you got _____ information?

5

I Correct the mistakes.

1 My sister she is a doctor. _____

2 'Have you got my bag?' 'Yes, I have got.' _____

3 He can't to use a computer. _____

4 I've got some luggages. _____

5 I'd like an advice. _____

5

TOTAL **50**

11 I'm reading a book

Present continuous

Positive		Negative		
I'm ('m = am)	reading.	I am not / I'm not		working.
He's/She's/It's ('s = is)		He/She/It	is not / isn't	
We're/You're/They're ('re = are)		We/You/They	are not / aren't	

I'm watching TV. (= *now*)   ▶▶ **Spelling page 64**
We're staying in a hotel. (= *temporary situation*)

A **Write present continuous sentences. Use short forms.**

1 I/come .... *I'm coming.* ....
2 it/begin ....
3 they/swim ....

4 we/move ....
5 you/not/go ....
6 she/not/stop ....

B **Look at the picture and complete the sentences in the present continuous. Use the verbs in the box.**

eat   drink   sit   wear   speak   read   ~~wear~~   work

1 The woman .... *is wearing* .... sunglasses.
2 She .... coffee.
3 She .... a book.
4 The man .... on the phone.
5 He .... a coat.
6 He .... a sandwich.
7 They .... at a café.
8 They .... in an office.

C **Write about what you are doing now.**

1 listen/to music ....
2 work/in an office ....
3 wear/jeans ....
4 drink/coffee ....
5 sit/on a train ....

12 Are you at home?

opposite	next to	near	between	in front of	behind

Go **to** the post office.

at	the bus stop / the supermarket / the airport / home
in	a taxi / England / Tokyo / bed
on	a bike / a bus / a train / a plane

A Underline the correct preposition.

1 She's working **in** / at Paris.

2 They're **to** / **at** the cinema.

3 Is he **in** / **at** / **to** home?

4 They're **to** / **at** / **on** the bus.

5 She's staying **at** / **in** / **to** bed today.

6 He's walking **at** / **to** the station.

B Look at the map and complete the sentences with a preposition.

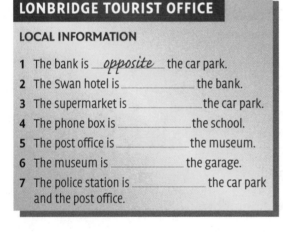

LONBRIDGE TOURIST OFFICE

LOCAL INFORMATION

1 The bank is _opposite_ the car park.

2 The Swan hotel is .... the bank.

3 The supermarket is .... the car park.

4 The phone box is .... the school.

5 The post office is .... the museum.

6 The museum is .... the garage.

7 The police station is .... the car park and the post office.

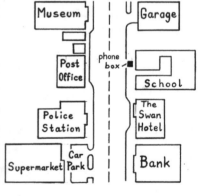

13 Is he working?

Present continuous

Question				Answer					
Am	I				I	am.		I'm not.	
Is	he/she/it	working?	Yes,		she	is.	No,	he	isn't.
Are	you/we/they				they	are.		we	aren't.
Where are they working?				In San Francisco.					

A It is Monday. Look at the planner for this London office and answer the questions.

Sales & Marketing Department				
	Mariella	**Mark**	**Luke**	**Kirsty**
Monday 1 May	Lisbon – visit client	New York – meet Director	sales conference	work at home
Tuesday 2 May	Lisbon			

1 Is Mariella working in the office? _No, she isn't._
2 What's Mark doing at the moment? _He's meeting the Director._
3 Is Kirsty working in New York? ....
4 Is Luke attending a sales conference? ....
5 Where's Mariella working? ....
6 What's she doing? ....
7 Who's meeting the Director? ....
8 Are Mark and Luke working at home? ....

B The people in the Sales and Marketing Department are speaking on the telephone. Write present continuous questions.

1 it snow/in New York, Mark? _Is it snowing in New York, Mark?_
2 the sun/shine/in Lisbon? ....
3 you/enjoy/life in London? ....
4 What/you/do, Kirsty? ....
5 Why/Mark/meet/the Director? ....
6 Who/attend/the sales conference? ....
7 you/speak/on a mobile phone? ....

14 We like our job

▶▶ Spelling page 64

Present simple

Positive			Negative		
I/You/We/They	start	at 8.00.	I/You/We/They	don't (=do not)	start at 7.00
He/She/It	starts		He/She/It	doesn't (=does not)	

Frequency adverbs

I **never/sometimes/usually/always** stay at home. (**not** I stay never)

A Complete the table with the correct form of the verb.

he/she/it		I/you/we/they	
positive	negative	positive	negative
1 *knows*	*doesn't know*	know	*don't know*
2		enjoy	
3	doesn't go		
4			don't use
5 has			
6		do	
7 works			
8		like	

B Underline the correct form.

1 I usually gets up / <u>I usually get up</u> at 6.00.

2 She usually reads / She reads usually the newspapers on Sunday.

3 I understand never / I never understand computers.

4 We like / We likes our job.

5 Never we stay / We never stay in four star hotels.

6 Always my sister works / My sister always works late.

C Complete the email with the verbs in the correct form of the present simple.

From: jsimmons
To: sbryant
Subject: Working schedules

Stephen

Here is the information you want.

Malcolm Benton (1) ___*comes*___ (come) in on Wednesdays and Thursdays. I (2) _____ (need) a red form for him, please. Andrea Rowe and Carol Harrison (3) _____ (work) late every Monday and Wednesday. They (4) _____ (leave) early on Friday mornings and they (5) _____ (not/come) in on Saturday mornings. Chris Kidman (6) _____ (have) one day off a week — Wednesday, I (7) _____ (think), or Thursday. Mark Davies and Stephanie Potter (8) _____ (get) two mornings off a week but I (9) _____ (not/know) which days — their manager (10) _____ (not/be) here at the moment. Stephanie (11) _____ (always/attend) management meetings on Mondays so I'll ask her.

Jane

D Write the verb in the present simple or present continuous.

HER KIND OF DAY

Megan is 81 years old. She (1) ___*is*___ (be) an actor and she (2) ___*lives*___ (live) in North London. Every day she (3) _____ (go) to the local swimming pool at 9.00 and (4) _____ (swim) a kilometer. Then she (5) _____ (do) the crossword in the newspaper and some gardening. At the moment she (6) _____ (work) four days a month on a TV programme so she (7) _____ (stay) in a hotel in the north of England. Every morning she (8) _____ (use) the hotel's open-air pool – even in the snow. Most nights Megan (9) _____ (listen) to the radio in bed because she (10) _____ (not sleep) very well.

15 You sound happy

Adjectives

common adjective endings		adjective + noun	verb + adjective		
-y	happy			feels	
-ing	interesting	It's a good film.	It	looks	good.
-ful	beautiful			sounds	
-ous	dangerous			tastes	

order:	**size +**	**age +**	**colour +**	**nationality +**	**noun**
a	small		green		coat
an		old		French	table

A **Are these right (✓) or wrong (✗)?**

1 heavy bags ....✓....   **2** reds flowers ....   **3** a big white car ....

4 It's an exercise easy. ....   **5** You look happy. ....   **6** She successful is. ....

B **Complete the adverts. Use a verb and an adjective.**

> **verbs:** ~~feel~~ taste feel look sound
> **adjectives:** ~~nervous~~ delicious young wonderful cold

1 Do you .....*feel nervous*........ about driving? Learn with *Pitstop* driving school.

2 Your CDs will .... on the new *Mitsonic* hi-fi system.

3 Paradise Pizzas .... !

4 You'll always .... with Capri make-up.

5 Don't .... this winter. *Skiwear100* has hats and gloves for everyone.

C **Write sentences with the adjectives in the correct place.**

1 We have teachers. (good)   *We have good teachers.*

2 Listen to this CD-player. (small/new) ....

3 Come to this restaurant. (Italian/big) ....

4 Try this lipstick. (pink/new) ....

5 We have sportswear. (American/modern) ....

16 Do you work too hard?

Present simple

Questions			Short answers					
Do	I/you/we/they	work?	Yes,	I/you/ we/they	do.	No,	I/you/ we/they	don't.
Does	he/she/it			he/she/it	does.		he/she/it	doesn't.
How much does it cost?			£5.00					
Where do you work?			In a bank.					

A Complete the questions in the quiz.

Do you work too hard?

1 *Do* you work 50+ hours a week?
2 .... you have lunch at your desk?
3 .... you often stay late at work?
4 .... you take work home every night?
5 .... your manager phone you at weekends?
6 .... people send you 20+ emails a day?
7 .... your manager send you faxes on holiday?
8 .... you always talk about work to friends?

6-8 ✓s = you work too hard - take a break!
3-5 ✓s = you work quite hard - don't do too much!
1-2 ✓s = you have time to relax after work - you're fine!

B Complete the quiz (✓ or ✗) for you.

C Now write short answers for you.

1 *Yes, I do. / No, I don't.*   5 ....
2 ....   6 ....
3 ....   7 ....
4 ....   8 ....

D Look at the answers in this job interview and complete the questions.

1 Where _do you work_ ?

I work for Loake's car dealers.

2 How many people _____ ?

I manage four people.

3 How many cars _____ in a week?

We usually sell about 30 cars.

4 What kind of car _____ ?

I drive a BMW.

5 _____ to other countries in your job?

No, I don't, but I travel a lot in the UK.

6 What _____ your manager _____ of you?

She thinks I'm a good worker.

7 How much holiday _____ your employers _____ you?

They give us 25 days' holiday a year.

8 How much _____ ?

I earn £20,000 a year.

E Complete the interviewer's report about the candidate. Use the present simple.

Candidate: Jack Amis

Interviewer: Alex Dane

Position applied for: Sales Manager

Mr Amis (1) _works_ for Loake's car dealers. He (2) _____ four people. He (3) _____ a BMW and he (4) _____ about 30 cars a week. He (5) _____ to other countries in his current job but he (6) _____ a lot in the UK. His employers (7) _____ him 25 days' holiday and he (8) _____ £20,000.

17 What do you do?

place	**Where's** Greenland? **Where** do you come from?
time	**When** does summer begin? **When's** your birthday?
things	**What's** your favourite film? **What** do you do?
people	**Who's** the leader of China? **Who's** your favourite writer?
reason	**Why** are CDs so expensive? **Why** are you learning languages?
method	**How** do you remember things? **How** do you get to work?
amount	**How much** do you earn? **How old** are you?

A Look at the poster and complete the questions with the words from the box.

~~who~~ how much where why how old what

1 _Who_ is this boy?
2 _____ musical instrument is he playing?
3 _____ is he wearing a uniform?
4 _____ is he? He looks very young.
5 _____ is he? Is he in a studio?
6 _____ does this poster cost?

B Write the questions with a question word. Then match the questions and answers.

1 the French/say 'I love you' _How do the French say 'I love you'?_ [f]
2 people/send Valentine cards? _____ [ ]
3 Cupid/carry/in the picture? _____ [ ]
4 Venus? _____ [ ]
5 we/say 'zero' in tennis? _____ [ ]
6 the Taj Mahal? _____ [ ]

a A bow and arrow. **b** On 14th February. **c** In India.
d The goddess of love in Roman mythology. **e** Love. **f** ~~Je t'aime.~~

18 I'm usually early

Frequency adverbs

never	sometimes		often		usually	always
0%						100%

Before the verb:
He **never arrives** late.
She doesn't **often arrive** late.
Do they **usually arrive** late?

After *be*:
He's **always** early.
She **isn't usually** early.
Are they **often** early?

ⓘ *Sometimes* and **usually** *can go at the beginning or end of a sentence:*
Sometimes/Usually she arrives early. They arrive early **sometimes/usually**.

ⓘ *Every day/month; once/twice a week; three times a year* *go at the end:*
She's early **every day**. They go on holiday **three times a year**.

A **Look at the survey and write the sentences about Dan.**

1 *He usually reads a newspaper.*
2
3
4
5
6

B **Write true sentences about you.**
Use the words in exercise A.

1 *I read a newspaper every day.*
2
3
4
5
6

Consumer Survey

Name: Dan Tuck

How often do you…

1 read a newspaper?

usually

2 watch TV?

three times a week

3 buy clothes?

sometimes

4 go on holiday?

once a year

5 eat in restaurants?

never

6 rent videos?

often

19 She learns quickly

Regular adverbs		Irregular adverbs	
adjective	**adverb +*ly***	**adjective**	**adverb**
beautiful	beautiful**ly**	good	well
slow	slow**ly**	fast	fast
quick	quick**ly**	hard	hard
adjective +*y*	**adverb +*ily***	late	late
happ**y**	happ**ily**	early	early
adjective +*ly*	**no adverb**		
friend**ly**	–		

ⓘ *These adverbs come after the main verb or after the verb + object:*
She learns **quickly**. She speaks English **well**.

A **Make adverbs from these adjectives.**

1 quick _quickly_ 2 good _____ 3 quiet _____

4 careful_____ 5 easy _____ 6 confident _____

7 clear _____ 8 late _____ 9 neat _____

10 hard _____ 11 early _____ 12 bad _____

B
Complete the sentences with an adverb from exercise A.

ADVICE FOR INTERVIEWEES

Arrive 15 minutes (1) _early_ for your interview. Never arrive
(2) _____. Dress (3) _____. Shake hands
(4) _____. Speak (5) _____ and think about your
answers (6) _____. Don't answer questions too
(7) _____.

C **Complete the sentences about you with an adverb.**

1 I speak _Italian well_ . 4 I work _____ .

2 I read _____ . 5 I learn _____ .

3 I write _____ . 6 I drive _____ .

20 I wasn't there

Past simple: *be*

Positive				Negative			
I/He/She/It	was	there yesterday.		I/He/She/It	wasn't	there yesterday.	
We/You/They	were			We/You/They	weren't		
Question				Answer			
Was	I/he/she/it	there yesterday?		Yes,	I/he/she/it	was.	
				No,		wasn't.	
Were	we/you/they			Yes,	we/you/they	were.	
				No,		weren't.	
Where were you yesterday?				I was at home.			

A Yesterday there was a robbery. Complete the police report with the past of positive *be*.

It (1) ___was___ a sunny day. There (2) _____
two robbers in the shop and one in a car outside. There
(3) _____ two men and one woman. The woman
(4) _____ in the shop. The men (5) _____ in
the car. Their car (6) _____ white.

B Complete the police questions for the answers in exercise A.

1 (___What was___ the weather like?

2 (_____ robbers _____ there?

3 (_____ they men or women?

4 (_____ the woman?

5 (_____ the men?

6 (_____ colour _____ their car?

C **Now look at the picture and correct the police report in exercise A.**

1 It _wasn't_ sunny. It _was_ rainy.

2 _____ two robbers in the shop. _____ three robbers in the shop.

3 _____ two men and one woman. _____ three men and one woman.

4 The woman _____ in the shop. She _____ in the car.

5 The men _____ in the car. They _____ in the shop.

6 Their car _____ white. It _____ black.

D **Complete the sentences about you.**

1 I _wasn't_ at home last night.

2 I _____ at work last Saturday.

3 It _____ sunny yesterday.

4 The shops _____ open yesterday.

5 My manager _____ in Brazil last year.

6 My friends and I _____ at the cinema last Friday.

Test 2 (Units 11-20)

A Circle the correct form.

1 'Where is he?' **'He's watching / He watches** TV.'

2 What **you are / are you** doing?

3 We live **at / in** Brazil.

4 He **doesn't / don't** like reading.

5 He **want / wants** a pizza.

6 Where **he lives / does he live**?

7 How many people **there are / are there**?

8 I **every day go to work / go to work every day**.

9 He's a **good driver / driver good**.

10 He drives **fast / fastly**.

| 10 |

B Write sentences in the present continuous.

1 He _____ . (swim)

2 _____ ? (it/rain)

3 Who _____ ? (she/meet)

4 What _____ ? (you/do)

5 They _____ . (not/leave)

| 5 |

C Write sentences in the present simple.

1 She _____ (teach) English.

2 He _____ (not/like) me.

3 When _____ (you/have) lunch?

4 When _____ (she/start) work?

5 They _____ (not/speak) English.

| 5 |

D Complete the sentences with a preposition.

1 Do you live _____ Japan?

2 She's _____ the bus stop.

3 I'm sitting _____ the bus.

4 She's staying _____ home today.

5 I'm going _____ Italy tomorrow.

| 5 |

E Write the verb in the present simple or present continuous.

1 Where _____ (you/work) at the moment?

2 Where _____ (you/usually/work)?

3 Oh, look at the weather! It _____ (rain).

4 _____ (you/have) dinner now?

5 She _____ (often/work) in Rome.

| 5 |

F Complete the questions.

1 '_____ are you?' 'I'm twenty-three.'

2 '_____ are you living now?' 'In Australia.'

3 '_____ does it cost?' 'Thirty dollars.'

4 '_____ do you like Salsa dancing?' 'Because it's fun.'

5 '_____ is he doing?' 'He's playing the piano.'

| 5 |

G Write a new sentence with the adverb or adjective.

1 He doesn't get up early. (always) _____

2 Sue's got a coat. (beautiful) _____

3 He goes to the cinema. (twice a week) _____

4 He's got a car. (red/big) _____

5 She works at the office. (hard/always) _____

| 5 |

H Complete the sentences with the correct past simple form of *be*.

1 She _____ (not) at home yesterday.

2 Where _____ you last week?

3 We _____ tired last night.

4 _____ he at the cinema last Friday?

5 _____ we early this morning?

| 5 |

I Correct the mistakes.

1 Where <u>they are</u> working today? _____

2 The bus stop is <u>in front</u> the hospital. _____

3 The station's <u>next</u> the garage. _____

4 He <u>gos</u> to college every day. _____

5 I feel <u>nervously</u>. _____

| 5 |

TOTAL | 50 |

21 They worked hard

Past simple

▶▶ Spelling page 64

Positive		Negative	
I/He/She/It/ We/You/They	worked.	I/He/She/It/ We/You/They	didn't work. (=did not)

A Read the article and underline the past tense verbs.

Hans Snook <u>grew up</u> in Canada. He went to university but he didn't finish his course and he didn't take a degree. He worked as the manager of a hotel in Vancouver and he met his wife, Etta, there. When he was 35 he left his job and he and Etta travelled around Asia. They didn't have much money and they only took their rucksacks. Hans had friends in Hong Kong and he got a job with them. He worked hard and only two years later he became the Director of Hutchison Hong Kong. He stayed there until 1993, when the company sent Hans to the UK. He started Orange, the successful UK mobile phone company. France Telecom bought the company for $36 billion in 2000. Hans didn't stay at Orange – he left and studied alternative medicine.

B Write the past simple verbs from exercise A in the box. Complete the positive and negative forms.

1 travel *travelled* *didn't travel*	2 start	3 grow up	4 go	5 take
6 leave	7 stay	8 meet	9 get	10 have
11 become	12 send	13 buy	14 study	15 finish

C Look at the CV and complete the sentences in the past simple.

CV

Lauren Minton

WORK

1996–now	Sales Rep, Nissan
1995–96	Waitress, Mango Restaurant, London
1994–95	South America

EDUCATION

1990–94	Edinburgh University
	BA Economics (1994)
1983–90	Lichfield School, London

---

1 She ___*went*___ to school in London. (go)
2 She ___*didn't leave*___ school in 1988. (leave)
3 She _____ school in 1990. (leave)
4 She _____ to Newcastle University. (go)
5 She _____ her degree in 1994. (take)
6 She _____ Economics. (study)
7 She _____ Art. (study)
8 She _____ around South America in 1994-95. (travel)
9 She _____ as a waitress in London. (work)

D Write past simple sentences about you. Use the verbs in the box.

~~go~~ leave study take travel work

1 ___*I went to school in Prague.*___
2 _____
3 _____
4 _____
5 _____
6 _____

	a/an	the
+ singular countable nouns	I've got **a** new **car**. (There are lots of cars. I've got one. You don't know which car.)	Where's **the car**? (You know which car.)

There's **a** book and **a** magazine on the table. **The** book is English and **the** magazine is Spanish. (*a* = first time; *the* = second time)

	no article	the
+ plural nouns + uncountable nouns	I like **jeans**. (=all/most jeans)	I like **the jeans** on the right.

ⓘ *The following have no article: Most countries* (Japan), *towns* (Moscow), *streets* (Wall Street), *continents* (Africa), *mountains* (Mount Fuji) *but we say*: the USA, the UK, the High Street. *We use* **the** *with seas* (the Pacific Ocean), *rivers* (the Amazon), *island groups* (the Bahamas), *mountain ranges* (the Alps) *and deserts* (the Sahara).

A Write *the* or nothing (**X**). Then match the questions and answers.

1 Where are *the* Himalayas?   **a** In .... Egypt.

2 Where is .... Sydney?   **b** In .... Atlantic Ocean.

3 Where is .... River Nile?   **c** Between .... Nepal and .... India.

4 Where are .... Canary Islands?   **d** In .... New York.

5 Where is .... Wall Street?   **e** In .... Australia.

6 Where is .... Mount Fuji?   **f** In .... UK.

7 Where are .... Shetland Islands?   **g** In .... Japan.

B Complete these newspaper extracts with *a*, *an*, *the* or nothing (**X**).

1 *The* Prime Minister visited *the* capital of **X** Paraguay last week.

2 .... Queen opened a new bridge across .... River Thames in London yesterday.

3 Tiger Woods won .... PGA Championship yesterday.

4 There was .... robbery in .... High Street on Friday.

5 .... President of .... USA will meet .... President of .... Zambia next week.

6 .... car crashed into .... train in .... India yesterday.

23 What did you see?

Past simple

Question			Answer		
Did	I/he/she/it/ we/you/they	go last night?	Yes,	I/he/she/it/ we/you/they	did.
			No,		didn't. (=did not)
What did you do yesterday?			I went to the cinema.		

Time expressions

on Monday 11 June	**in** the morning April 2000	**at** 6 o'clock the weekend	**last** night week month	three years two days a week	**ago** (=before now)

A **Complete the questions with the past simple. Use the verbs in the box.**

> buy   cost   eat   go   leave   meet   ~~see~~

1 I went to the cinema last night.
    What _did you see?_

2 We had dinner at that new restaurant last Tuesday.
    What ....

3 I bought these shoes yesterday.
    How much ....

4 My sister went on holiday last weekend.
    Where ....

5 I met a famous actor last night.
    Who ....

6 Kate and Matt stayed really late at my party.
    When ....

7 I went shopping yesterday afternoon.
    What ....

B Complete the questions with *when* and the past simple. Use the verbs in the box.

| become   die   leave   ~~make~~   start   walk   win |

1 *When did* .... Levi Strauss ..... *make* ..... the first jeans?
2 .... Neil Armstrong .... on the moon?
3 .... Boris Yeltsin .... President of Russia?
4 .... Mahatma Gandhi ....?
5 .... the British .... Hong Kong?
6 .... Nelson Mandela .... the Nobel peace prize?
7 .... the United Nations ....?

C Underline the correct preposition. Then match the answers with the questions in exercise B.

a **In / On / At** 1991. ....
b **In / On / At** 21st July 1969. ....
c <u>**In**</u> / **On** / **At** 1923. .....*1*.....
d **In / On / At** October 1945. ....
e **In / On / At** 1993. ....
f **In / On / At** Tuesday 1st July 1997. ....
g **In / On / At** 30th January 1948. ....

D Complete the sentences about you. Use the past simple.

1 *I went to China last* ..... April.
2 .... year.
3 .... 1998.
4 .... Monday.
5 .... ago.
6 .... 7 o'clock this morning.

24 I'm going to stop the car!

Going to

Positive			Negative		
I'm		going to arrive tomorrow.	I	am not	going to leave tomorrow.
He's/She's/It's			He/She/It	isn't	
We're/You're/They're			We/You/They	aren't	

Questions			Answers						
Am	I	going to stay next week?	Yes,	I	am.	No,	I'm not		
Is	he/she/it			he/she/it	is.		he/she/it	isn't.	
Are	you			you	are.		you	aren't.	
What is she going to do?			She's going to make a phone call.						

ⓘ *We use **going to** when we can see what is certain to happen or we have a plan.*
Look at those clouds. It's going to rain.
We're going to paint the bathroom tomorrow.

A Complete the sentences in B with *going to*. Then match the
sentences in A and B.

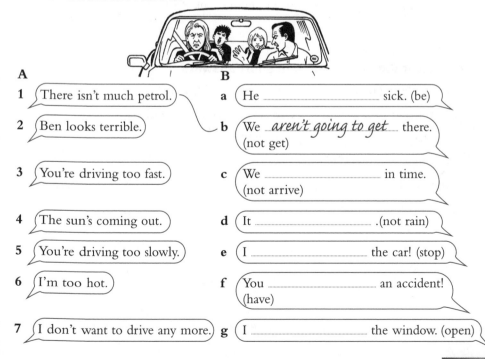

A

1 There isn't much petrol.

2 Ben looks terrible.

3 You're driving too fast.

4 The sun's coming out.

5 You're driving too slowly.

6 I'm too hot.

7 I don't want to drive any more.

B

a He _____ sick. (be)

b We *aren't going to get* there. (not get)

c We _____ in time. (not arrive)

d It _____ . (not rain)

e I _____ the car! (stop)

f You _____ an accident! (have)

g I _____ the window. (open)

B Complete the questions to ask for more information. Use a question word from the box and *going to*.

> where   how much   ~~what~~   what   who   why

1 — I'm going to see a film tomorrow.

What are you going to see?

2 — Jon's going to make dinner this evening.

.... cook?

3 — Leila and Chris are going to have a holiday this summer.

.... go?

4 — I'm going to make a phone call in a minute.

.... phone?

5 — Ivan is going to leave his job next month.

.... leave?

6 — I'm going to get some money from the bank.

.... get?

C Answer the questions. Use short answers.

1 Are you going to phone anyone tonight? *Yes, I am.*

2 Are you and your friends going to watch a video tonight? ....

3 Is a friend going to visit you at the weekend? ....

4 Are you going to get up early tomorrow? ....

5 Are the Olympic Games going to take place in 2012? ....

6 Is your country going to have an election next year? ....

25 Is there any soap?

some (+positive)				
uncountable nouns	There	is	some	water.
plural nouns		are		aspirins.

ⓘ *We also use **some** in offers and requests:*

offer: Would you like some water?

request: Can/Could I have some shampoo?

any (+negatives and questions)						
uncountable nouns	There	isn't	any	soap.	Is	there any	soap?
plural nouns		aren't		tissues.	Are		tissues?

A Match the beginning of each sentence with its correct ending.

1 Would you like a
    a cough medicine?
    b large or small bottle?

2 There's
    a throat sweets on the shelf.
    b baby oil on the shelf.

3 Can I have some
    a toothpaste?
    b large box of plasters?

4 There isn't any
    a reading glasses.
    b soap.

5 Could I have some
    a suncream?
    b large bottle of aspirins?

6 Are there any
    a shampoo?
    b stomach pills?

B Complete the sentences with *a*, *an*, *some* or *any*.

1 There aren't ___any___ stomach pills.

2 There isn't _____ bath oil, I'm afraid.

3 What about _____ box of tissues?

4 Would you like _____ aspirins or paracetamol?

5 Can I have _____ cough medicine, please?

6 I'd like _____ bottle of shampoo.

7 We don't have _____ face cream.

8 Could I have _____ tissues?

26 I have to get up early

Positive			Negative		
I/You/ We/They	have to	go.	I/You/ We/They	don't have to	go.
He/She/It	has to		He/She/It	doesn't have to	
Question			Answer		
Do	I/you/ we/they	have to go?	Yes,	I/you/we/they	do.
			No,		don't.
Does	he/she/it		Yes,	he/she/it	does.
			No,		doesn't.

ⓘ *Necessary*: I have to get up early for work.
Not necessary: I don't have to get up early at the weekend.

A Look at the information about the law in Germany and Australia. Complete the sentences with *have to* and the verb.

	Germany	Australia
carry an identity card	yes	no
vote in a general election	no	yes
stay at school	yes – until age 18	yes – until age 15–16

1 In Germany, people ___*have to carry*___ an identity card.
2 In Australia, people _____ an identity card.
3 In Germany, people _____ in a general election.
4 In Australia, people _____ in a general election.
5 In Germany, children _____ at school until they are 18.
6 In Australia, children _____ at school until they are 18.

B Complete the sentences with *have to* and a verb from the box.

| look after   work   drive   ~~keep~~   wear   get up   speak |

1 Firefighters *have to keep* fit.
2 Police officers _____ a uniform.
3 A nurse _____ long hours.
4 International pilots _____ English.
5 A lorry driver _____ long distances.
6 Postal workers _____ early.
7 A vet _____ animals.

C Write questions with *have to* about Pavel's job. Look at the answers. Which job in exercise B does he do?

1 he/work in an office?
Does he have to work in an office?   No, he doesn't.

2 he/work at night?
_____?   Yes, he does.

3 people in his job/wear a suit?
_____?   No, they don't.

4 he/wear a uniform?
_____?   Yes, he does.

5 people in his job/speak English?
_____?   Yes, they do.

6 he/work long hours?
_____?   Yes, he does.

7 people in his job/keep fit?
_____?   Yes, they do.

D Answer the questions about your country. Use short answers.

1 Do you have to carry an identity card? _____
2 Do people have to vote in a general election? _____
3 Do children have to stay at school until they are 18? _____
4 Do children have to stay at school until they are 16? _____
5 Do you have to have a visa to visit the UK? _____
6 Does a driver have to take driving exams every year? _____

27 Let's go out

Suggestion			Response
Let's Shall I/we Why don't we/you	go	out?	Good idea. OK.
What about	going		

A Circle the correct form.

1 Shall we (go) / going by car?
2 What about take / taking a taxi?
3 Let's walk / walking.
4 Shall I cycle / cycling?
5 What about catch / catching the train?
6 Shall we get / getting the bus?
7 Let's stay / staying at home.

B Complete the sentences with the verb in the correct form.

1 Let's ......*go*...... out for a meal. (go)
  What about ...*trying*... the new Indian restaurant? (try)

2 What about ....a football match? (see)
  Shall we ....this Saturday? (go)

3 Let's .... a show in London. (see)
  No, I'm too tired. What about .... to the cinema? (go)

4 Let's try to .... into the exhibition. (get)
  Why don't we .... early in the morning? (go)

5 Shall I .... tickets for *Hamlet*? (get)
  Why don't you .... them a ring? (give)

28 How much fruit do you eat?

	Countable	Uncountable
Question	How **many** eggs do you eat? **A lot.** **Not many.** **None.**	How **much** fish do you eat? **A lot.** **Not much.** **None.**
Positive	I eat **a lot of** eggs.	I eat **a lot of** fish.
Negative	I don't eat **many/any** chips.	I don't eat **much/any** meat.

A Look at Tom's questionnaire. Complete the sentences about him.

1 He _doesn't eat many_ sweets.
2 He _eats a lot of_ biscuits.
3 He .... chocolate.
4 He .... ice-cream.
5 He .... vegetables.
6 He .... brown rice.
7 He .... fruit.
8 He .... brown bread.

What do you eat?

	a lot	not much/ not many	none
1 sweets	☐	☑	☐
2 biscuits	☑	☐	☐
3 chocolate	☐	☐	☑
4 ice-cream	☐	☑	☐
5 vegetables	☐	☑	☐
6 brown rice	☐	☐	☑
7 fruit	☑	☐	☐
8 brown bread	☐	☐	☑

B Now write sentences for you.

1 I .... chocolate.
2 I .... biscuits.
3 I .... ice-cream.
4 I .... vegetables.
5 I .... fruit.
6 I .... brown bread.

C Write more questions about what we eat and drink a day for the questionnaire. Use _how much_ or _how many_.

1 (coffee) _How much coffee do you drink?_
2 (glasses of water) ....
3 (cheese) ....
4 (eggs) ....
5 (tomatoes) ....
6 (milk) ....

29 It's more expensive

	Adjective	Comparative
Short adjectives ➤➤ Spelling page 64	cold	colder
Adjectives ending in -y	happy	happier
Long adjectives	interesting	more interesting
Irregular adjectives	good	better
	bad	worse

My brother is **older than** me. His job is **more interesting than** mine.

A Write the comparative form of these adjectives.

1 cheap _cheaper_   2 important ....   3 easy ....

4 difficult ....   5 young ....   6 expensive ....

7 tall ....   8 fast ....   9 heavy ....

10 big ....   11 modern ....   12 good ....

B Use comparatives to complete the telephone company's report.

Our company is (1) _bigger_ (big) than last year and it is (2) ....
(good) than Quickcall International. We sell phones (3) .... (fast)
than they do and our phones are (4) .... (modern) than theirs.
Quickcall phones are (5) .... (difficult) to use than ours. Our
customers are (6) .... (happy) than Quickcall's customers.

C Use comparatives to write about the cameras.

Penton
• weight: 850g
• price: $800
• zoom lens

Canax
• weight: 300g
• price: $100

1   _The Canax camera is cheaper than the Penton._

2 ....

3 ....

4 ....

5 ....

30 The biggest in the world

	Adjective	Superlative
Short adjectives ▶▶ **Spelling page 64**	cold	the cold**est**
Adjectives ending in *-y*	happy	the happ**iest**
Long adjectives	interesting	**the most** interesting
Irregular adjectives	good	the best
	bad	the worst

The Pacific is **the biggest** ocean in the world. (*=It is bigger than all the others.*)

A Write the superlative form of these adjectives.

1 bad _____*the worst*_____ 2 short _____ 3 fast _____

4 interesting _____ 5 expensive _____ 6 heavy _____

7 long _____ 8 big _____ 9 dangerous _____

B Complete the sentences with a superlative from exercise A.

AMAZING FACTS

1 The *heaviest* baby in the world was 10.2 kg, born in Italy in 1995.
2 The _____ woman was only 61 cm tall and lived in New York City.
3 The world's _____ omelette had 160,000 eggs.
4 The _____ meal cost $21,000 for three people in London in 1997.
5 The _____ bridge is in Louisiana, USA. It is over 38 km long.
6 The _____ fish is the sailfish. It can swim 109 km/h.

C Use superlatives to write sentences about you and your family.

1 (young) _____*I am the youngest person in my family.*_____
2 (tall) _____
3 (intelligent) _____
4 (good singer) _____
5 (old) _____
6 (short) _____

Test 3 (Units 21-30)

A **Circle the correct form.**

1 What **he did** / **did he** do?

2 I didn't go home **last night** / **on yesterday night**.

3 My birthday's **in** / **on** July.

4 Who **you are** / **are you** going to meet tonight?

5 I **don't have to** / **haven't to** wear a suit at work.

6 Shall we **go** / **going** to the party?

7 **How much** / **How many** eggs would you like?

8 What about **to get** / **get** / **getting** a bus?

9 My car's **more fast** / **faster** than yours.

10 Your bag's **heavier** / **more heavy** than mine.

10

B **Write *the* or nothing (✗).**

1 Please clean .... car.

2 I live in .... Moscow.

3 What's .... fastest animal?

4 How big is .... Atlantic Ocean?

5 Do you eat .... meat?

5

C **Write questions. Use the form in brackets.**

1 where/you/eat later? (*going to*) ....

2 she/play/tennis? (*going to*) ....

3 he/get up early everyday? (*have to*) ....

4 what exams/you/take? (*have to*) ....

5 you/be/a teacher? (*going to*) ....

5

D **Write the verbs in the past simple.**

1 get ....

2 have ....

3 leave ....

4 see ....

5 buy ....

5

E **Write the verbs in the correct form.**

1 She (work) _____ for Honda in 1996.
2 We (not/see) _____ the film last night.
3 Where (you/go) _____ yesterday?
4 Look at those black clouds. It (rain) _____ soon.
5 I love animals. I (be) _____ a vet when I grow up.

| 5 |

F **Write *ago, last, yesterday, in, on* or *at*.**

1 The bus leaves _____ 6 o'clock.
2 Is there a train _____ the morning?
3 Your plane left 10 minutes _____ !
4 I saw him _____ morning.
5 Let's play tennis _____ Monday.

| 5 |

G **Write *much, many* or *a lot (of)*.**

1 How _____ milk is there?
2 How _____ eggs are there?
3 I eat _____ bread.
4 I don't eat _____ fruit.
5 I don't eat _____ sweets.

| 5 |

H **Complete the sentences with a comparative or superlative form.**

1 She's much _____ her brother. (young)
2 He's _____ in the class. (old)
3 The Regent Hotel is _____ the Crown Hotel. (expensive)
4 This hotel is _____ hotel in Sydney! (expensive)
5 What is _____ country in the world? (hot)

| 5 |

I **Correct the mistakes.**

1 They lived in <u>United States</u>. _____
2 I don't like <u>picture</u> on the right. _____
3 She's <u>going watch</u> TV. _____
4 He <u>not have to</u> worry. _____
5 Shall I <u>to open</u> the window? _____

| 5 |

TOTAL | 50 |

31 I like studying

Verb	+ verb-*ing*	Verb	+ *to* + verb
I love enjoy like hate	**travelling**. **studying**.	I hope/love/like want/hate would like (= I'd like) would love (= I'd love)	**to travel**. **to study**.

A Circle the correct form.

1 Music Lessons
Would you like (to play) / playing the piano in only 6 hours?

2 Radio Maxim 101
Enjoy **listening / to listen** to your favourite music on 101 FM.

3 Language courses
Do you want **speaking / to speak** a new language?

4 Video central
For everyone who would love **to watch / watching** great films.

5 Buydirect.com
Do you hate **waiting / wait** at the supermarket checkout?
Buy your shopping on the internet at Buydirect.com.

B Complete the email with the correct form of the verbs.

Thanks for the invitation. I'd love (1) __to see__ (see) you again and Sarah wants (2) _____ (visit) Glasgow. We'd like (3) _____ (come) next weekend. Is that OK? Sarah hates (4) _____ (drive), so we hope (5) _____ (come) by train.

There's an exhibition at the Gallery of Modern Art on Sunday and we'd like (6) _____ (go). We like (7) _____ (walk) around art galleries and (8) _____ (look) at pictures. Hope (9) _____ (see) you soon!

C Complete the sentences about you. Use verb + *-ing* or *to* + verb.

1 I love *going out with friends* _____ .

2 I'd like _____ next week.

3 I enjoy _____ .

4 I want _____ tomorrow.

5 I hate _____ .

6 I'd love _____ for my next birthday.

32 She hasn't visited Japan

Present perfect

▶▶ Spelling page 64

Positive		Negative		
I've/You've/We've/They've ('ve = have)	visited India.	I/You/We/They	haven't (=have not)	visited India.
He's/She's/It's ('s = has)		He/She/It	hasn't (=has not)	

ⓘ *We don't say when:* I've lived in Japan. (**not** ~~I've lived in Japan in 1998~~)
I've never lived in Poland. (never = at no time.)

A Look at the passports. Write sentences in the present perfect.

1 He/travel/Australia *He hasn't travelled to Australia.*
2 He/travel/Brazil ....
3 They/travel/Kenya ....
4 She/travel/Russia ....
5 They/travel/Singapore ....
6 She/travel/Poland ....

B Complete the sentences with the present perfect.

1 I *'ve walked up* .... Sugar Loaf mountain. (walk)
2 I .... football in the Maracanã. (watch)
3 I .... in St Petersburg. (study)
4 We .... Nairobi National Park. (visit)
5 I .... in the Ritz Hotel. (never, stay)
6 We .... in Singapore. (never, live)

C Write sentences about you.

1 I *'ve stayed / haven't stayed* in a lot of luxury hotels. (stay)
2 I .... in New Zealand. (live)
3 I .... a lot. (travel)
4 I .... a famous person for a meal. (invite)
5 I .... Indian food. (try)
6 I .... Scotland. (visit)

33 The train's just left

Present perfect	Some irregular verbs	
	Verb	Past participle
I've **cut** my finger. It's bleeding.	cut	cut
The train's **left**. I can't get home.	leave	left
She's **broken** her leg. She can't walk.	break	broken

ⓘ *We can use the present perfect for things in the near past with a result now.*

just	yet (with negatives and questions)
The train's **just** left. (= a short time before now)	The train hasn't left **yet**. (= but I expect it to leave soon.)

A Match the verbs with the past participles in the box.

> given eaten met ~~lost~~ seen made been done taken had

1 lose ___lost___ **2** give___ **3** eat___ **4** see___ **5** meet___
6 have___ **7** take___ **8** make___ **9** be (go)___ **10** do___

B Look at the pictures and complete the sentence with *just* and a verb from exercise A. Use the present perfect.

1 We*'ve just made* some biscuits.

2 I ___ to the shops.

3 He ___ my sandwich!

4 They ___ me a present.

5 She ___ my bag!

6 I ___ a shower.

C Look at the minutes of the meeting. What have people done?
What haven't they done yet? Write present perfect sentences.

Meeting 25 March 2002
Action points:
(Mara meet Director)
(Andy and Yama meet Exton sales people)
Mahmoud give new CD-ROMs to Kate ✓
(Yoriko see Sales Manager)
Yama make a new list of customers ✓
(Dan take new designs to Tokyo office)

1 Mara/the Director
Mara hasn't met the Director yet.

2 Andy and Yama/the Exton sales people

3 Mahmoud/the new CD-ROMs to Kate

4 Yoriko/the Sales Manager

5 Yama/a new list of customers

6 Dan/the new designs to the Tokyo office

D Write present perfect sentences about what you've done
today. Use the verb and *just* or *yet* where necessary.

1 (eat) *I haven't eaten lunch yet.*
2 (do)
3 (write)
4 (see)
5 (make)
6 (have)

34 Is it a long way?

What time is **it**?	**It's** three o'clock.
What day is **it**?	**It's** Thursday.
What date is **it**?	**It's** 14th December.
What's the weather like?	**It's** snowing. / **It's** windy. / **It's** sunny.
How far is **it** from Scotland to Iceland?	**It's** 798 kilometres.
Is **it** a long way?	Yes, **it** is. / No, **it** isn't.

A Look at the pictures. Write sentences with *it*.

1 *It's 12 July.*

2 ....

3 ....

4 ....

5 ....

6 ....

B Look at the weather map and complete the sentences.

1 *It's raining* in London.

2 .... in Spain.

3 .... in Italy.

4 .... in France.

5 .... January.

6 .... o'clock.

....07.00 19 January......

C Answer the questions. Use *it*.

1 What's the time now? .... *It's 1 o'clock.*

2 How far is it from your house to work? ....

3 What's the weather like today? ....

4 Is it a long way from England to your country? ....

5 What day of the week is it today? ....

6 What's the date today? ....

35 Have you finished?

Present perfect

Question			Answer		
Have	I/you/we/they	finished?	Yes, No,	I/you/we/they	have. haven't.
Has	he/she/it		Yes, No,	he/she/it	has. hasn't.

ever (+ questions) = *at any time*: **Have** you **ever flown** with Aeroflot?

yet (+ negatives and questions) = *for things we expect*: **Has** our bus **left yet**?

already = *earlier than we expect*: Has the train **already arrived**?

A Write questions for an interview and write short answers for you.

1 ever/live/abroad? *Have you ever lived abroad?*   *No, I haven't.*

2 ever/be/to Australia? ....

3 study/finance? ....

4 take/exams in Accountancy? ....

5 have/a job in a big company? ....

6 ever/work/with a lot of people? ....

B Write questions. Look at the timetable and write the answers.

TIME	TRAIN DEPARTURES			
16:50	STOKE 16·40	YORK 16·45	PERTH 16·55	HULL 17·00

1 the York train/leave/yet? *Has the York train left yet?* *Yes, it has.*

2 I/miss/the train for Hull?

3 the train for Perth/
already/leave?

4 we/miss/the train for Stoke?

5 the Stoke and York
trains/leave/yet?

6 I/miss/the train for Perth?

36 Send me the bill

	Verb	+ object 1	+ object 2	Common verbs with 2 objects:		
Can you	buy give bring send	me her	a postcard? a book? some flowers?	cook make show tell	get pass take write	lend read teach

I got my sister a present. = *I got a present for my sister.*

A Rewrite the sentences without *to* or *for*.

1 Can you get some stamps for me? _*Can you get me some stamps?*_
2 Can you send this letter to my son? ....
3 She showed the postcard to us. ....
4 Can you send the bill to me? ....
5 Please buy a pen for me. ....
6 He cooked a meal for her. ....

B Look at this present list and complete the sentences.

1 He didn't get _*his mother a pair of gloves.*_ (mother)
2 He gave .... (Mark)
3 He took .... (mother)
4 He didn't buy .... (Karen)
5 He sent .... (Jane)
6 He got .... (Karen)
7 He didn't give .... (Mark)

PRESENTS

Mum - a pair of gloves
a watch
Karen - a guitar
a mobile phone
Mark - a camera
a video
Jane - some chocolates

C Write the words in the correct order to make sentences.

1 (time tell me the you can ?) _*Can you tell me the time?*_
2 (buy a can drink you her ?) ....
3 (money him lent I some .) ....
4 (this please letter me read .) ....
5 (cooked a great meal her I .) ....
6 (salt you the pass can me .) ....

37 I was having dinner

Past continuous

Positive			Negative		
I/He/She/it	was	working last night.	I/He/She/It	wasn't (=was not)	watching TV.
We/You/They	were		We/You/They	weren't (=were not)	

At 8.30 yesterday I was having dinner. *(I started at 8.00 and finished at 9.00.)*

A Complete the newspaper article with the past continuous.

At 8pm last night there was an explosion in Warren Road in London. It (1) *was raining* (rain) and people (2) _____ (sit) in cafés. People (3) _____ (do) some late shopping. Jane Glover described what happened: 'I (4) _____ (wait) at the bus stop and I saw this man. He (5) _____ (wear) sunglasses and he (6) _____ (carry) a big black bag. Two minutes later there was a loud bang.'

B People are answering a police officer's questions about the explosion. Complete the sentences.

1 I wasn't near Warren Road. I *was driving* (drive) to Manchester.

2 My friends and I _____ (watch) the football match on TV.

3 My girlfriend _____ (have) dinner in a restaurant with me.

4 I _____ (work) in my uncle's shop.

5 I _____ (not/stay) in London last night.

6 My children _____ (not/feel) well so I was at home with them.

C Write sentences about you. Use the past continuous.

1 At 6 o'clock yesterday morning, I _____

2 At 7 o'clock yesterday morning, I _____

3 At 12 o'clock yesterday morning, I _____

4 At 3 o'clock yesterday afternoon, I _____

5 At 8 o'clock yesterday evening, I _____

38 I'll help you

*We use **will** when:*
    we decide now: The phone's ringing. I'll answer it.
    we make offers, requests, promises: I'll help you. **Will** you open the door, please?
    we predict the future: This horse **will** win the race tomorrow.

*We use **going to** when:*
    we decide before now (= a plan): I'm **going to** paint the room. I've got the paint.
    we can see now what is certain to happen: The horse in front **is going to** win.

ⓘ *Sometimes we can use both **will** and **going to**:*
    It **won't** rain. = It **isn't going to** rain.
    I'll be 30 next year. = I'm **going to** be 30 next year.

A Complete the messages with *will* or *going to*.

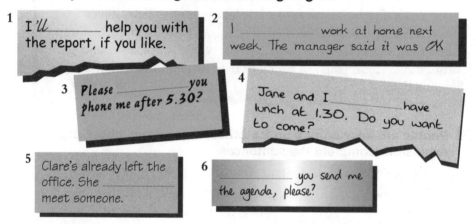

1 I 'll_____ help you with the report, if you like.

2 I _____ work at home next week. The manager said it was OK

3 Please _____ you phone me after 5.30?

4 Jane and I _____ have lunch at 1.30. Do you want to come?

5 Clare's already left the office. She _____ meet someone.

6 _____ you send me the agenda, please?

B Complete the sentences. Use positive or negative *will* or *going to*.

1 'The phone's ringing.' '(I/answer) ___I'll answer___ it.'

2 'Where are my car keys?' 'I've got them. (I/take) _____ the car to the garage.'

3 'Please be on time.' 'Don't worry. (I/be) _____ late.'

4 'Jack's just got a new job.' 'What company (he/work) _____ for?'

5 'It's cold in here. Is the window open?' 'OK, (I/close) _____ it.'

6 'What's the time?' 'I don't know. Ask Amy. (She/tell) _____ you.'

7 'There's a film on TV tonight.' 'I know, but I'm really tired so (I/watch) _____ it.'

39 Were you working?

Past continuous

Was	I/he/he/it		Yes,	I/he/she/it	was.
		working at 6 pm yesterday?	No,		wasn't.
Were	we/you/they		Yes,	we/you/they	were.
			No,		weren't.

What was he doing at 7 o'clock?

A These are pictures from office security cameras at 10 am yesterday. Answer the questions.

1 Was the Manager using his computer? ...... *No, he wasn't.*

2 What was he doing? ......

3 Were the receptionists speaking on the phone? ......

4 What were they doing? ......

5 Was the Director having a meeting in her office? ......

6 Was she sitting down? ......

B Complete the past continuous questions and write your answers.

1 (you/work) *Were you working* at 6 o'clock last night? ...... *Yes, I was.*

2 Where (you/live) ...... in October 2001? ......

3 (you/study) ...... English this time last year? ......

4 Where (your best friend/live) ...... five years ago? ......

5 (it/rain) ...... when you woke up yesterday morning? ......

6 What (you/do) ...... on 31 December 1999? ......

40 If I finish, I'll ...

when/if	Present simple	Future	
When	I finish the course	I'll I'm going to	have a party.
If	I finish the course	I'll	have a party.

When I finish = *I know I'll finish*
If I finish = *it's possible I'll finish (I don't know)*

ⓘ *We say*: When/If **I finish**... (**not** ~~When/If I'll finish~~...).

When I **leave** work next year, **I'm going to** travel around Africa.
When I **leave** work next year, **I'll** travel around Africa.

A Write the verbs in the correct form. Both *will* and *going to* are
possible for the future.

1 When I _____*finish*_____ (finish) my exams next year, I *'m going to leave*
(leave) university.

2 When I _____ (leave) university, I _____ (travel)
around South America.

3 When I _____ (return), I _____ (work) for a small
design company in London.

4 When I _____ (finish) my contract, I _____ (find)
another job.

5 I _____ (apply) for an Australian work visa when
I _____ (be) 26.

6 When I _____ (get) to Australia, I _____ (look) for
a job in Sydney.

B Complete the answers to a student's questions.

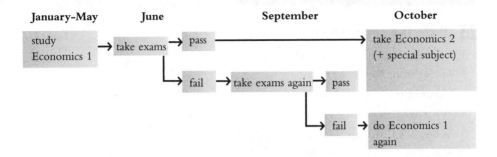

January–May	June		September	October
study Economics 1	→ take exams →	pass	——————————→	take Economics 2 (+ special subject)
		↳ fail → take exams again →	pass	
			↳ fail →	do Economics 1 again

1   *If you take*   (take) this course, you *'ll study*   (study)
Economics 1 and 2.

2   _____ (pass) the exams in June, you _____ (do)
Economics 2 in October.

3   _____ (take) Economics 2, you _____ (study)
a special subject.

4   _____ (fail) the exams in June, you _____ (take)
them again in September.

5   You _____ (do) Economics 1 again if _____ (fail)
the exams in September.

6   _____ (pass) the exams in September, you _____
(study) Economics 2.

C Complete the sentences about you.

1 When I'm older, _____ .
2 When I wake up tomorrow, _____ .
3 If the weather _____ tomorrow, _____ .
4 When _____, I'll travel _____ .
5 I'll be very happy if _____ .

Test 4 (Units 31-40)

A Circle the correct form.

1 I like **go** / **going** out for dinner.
2 **Is** / **It's** not very cold today.
3 She told **me** / **to me** a story.
4 What **was she** / **she was** doing at 7 o'clock?
5 When **it's** / **it'll be** summer, I'll go on holiday.
6 She enjoys to **read** / **reading**.
7 **I went** / **I've been** to Thailand last year.
8 Can you get **me** / **for me** a glass of milk?
9 I'd love **to have** / **having** a cold drink.
10 How far **is** / **is it** from here to the station?

| 10 |

B Write sentences in the present perfect.

1 she/never/live/in Greece
2 they/have/dinner/already?
3 our bus/leave/yet?
4 they/not/eat/lunch/yet
5 I/not/lose/it

| 5 |

C Write sentences in the past continuous.

1 it/rain
2 she/not/look
3 they/work?
4 what/he/do?
5 who/they/meet?

| 5 |

D Write the verbs in the correct form.

1 I hope (see) _____ you soon.
2 She wants (have) _____ a party.
3 I hate (get up) _____ .
4 Do you like (work) _____ here?
5 Would you like (go) _____ out?

| 5 |

E Complete the sentences with *'ll* or *going to* in the correct form.

1 I _____ see you later. OK?
2 Please be quiet. The film_____ start.
3 Why _____ (he) work in Spain?
4 _____ (you) close the door, please?
5 I'm busy tomorrow. I _____ see a film.

5

F Write the verbs in the correct form.

1 When I (go) _____ to the party tomorrow, I (wear) _____
my new dress.
2 If I (see) _____ her next week, I (tell) _____ her.
3 I saw your brother yesterday. He (stand) _____ at the bus stop.
4 (you/have) _____ lunch yet?
5 The train (already/leave) _____ . It went ten
minutes ago.

5

G Write the words in the correct order to make a sentence.

1 eaten food have ever you Thai ?_____
2 present gave I a her ._____
3 letter you me write a did ?_____
4 way it long is a ?_____
5 working year she last was where ?_____

H Correct the mistakes.

5

1 I <u>want have</u> a holiday _____
2 How far <u>is</u> from London to Paris?_____
3 I <u>enjoy to swim</u>. _____
4 If the bus <u>will be</u> late, we'll walk. _____
5 I'll ring you when I'<u>ll get</u> there. _____

5

I Write the past participle of these verbs.

1 eat_____
2 cut _____
3 break _____
4 give _____

5

5 lose _____

TOTAL **50**

Spelling

Unit 11: verb +*ing*

verb ends in *e*:	~~e~~ +*ing*	verb ends in *ie*:	~~ie~~ +*ying*
make	→ making	lie	lying
write	→ writing		

verb ends in 1 vowel + 1 consonant:		verb ends in 2 vowels + 1 consonant:	
sit	→ sitting	read	→ reading
run	→ running	wear	→ wearing

Unit 14: verb +*s*, +*es*

verb:	+*s*	verb ends –*ch*/-*sh*/-*ss*/-*x*/-*o*:	+*es*
work	→ works	teach	→ teaches
start	→ starts	wash	→ washes
need	→ needs	do	→ does

irregular verbs:		verb ends in consonant + *y*:	~~y~~ +*ies*
have	→ has	study	→ studies
be	→ is	fly	→ flies

Unit 21, 32: verb +*ed*

verb +*ed*		start	→ started
verb ends in –*e*: +*d*		like	→ liked
verb ends in consonant + *y*: ~~y~~ +*ied*		carry	→ carried
one-syllable verb, ends in 1 vowel + 1 consonant:		stop	→ stopped
		drop	→ dropped
two-syllable verb, ends in 1 vowel + 1 consonant:		travel	→ travelled

Unit 29, 30: adjective +*er*, +*est*

one-syllable adjective, ends in one vowel + one consonant:			
hot	→ hotter, hottest	big	→ bigger, biggest

two-syllable adjective, ends in –*y*:		~~y~~ +*ier*/+*iest*	
happy	→ happier, happiest	pretty	→ prettier, prettiest

ⓘ vowels: a e i o u; consonants: b c d f g h j k l m n p q r s t v w x y z
one-syllable words: work, start, big
two-syllable words: travel (trav+el), begin (be+gin), pretty (pre+tty)

Answer key

Unit 1
A 2 No, it isn't. (No, it's not.) 3 Yes, he is.
  4 Yes, they are.
  5 No, he isn't. (No, he's not.)
  6 No, they aren't. (No, they're not.)

B 2 Is Euromett a Polish company?
    No, it isn't. (No, it's not.)
  3 Are Advanta's offices in São Paulo?
    Yes, they are.
  4 Is Mr Al Zahrani an accountant?
    Yes, he is.
  5 Is KBS's web page www.yukie.com?
    No, it isn't. (No, it's not.)
  6 Are Mr Melo and Mr Zahrani from
    Germany?
    No, they aren't. (No, they're not.)

C 2 'm … 'm … 3 is … 's 4 are
  5 're 6 's 7 's

D 2 isn't ('s not) 3 'm not 4 aren't ('re not)
  5 isn't ('s not) 6 isn't ('s not)

E Answers will vary.

Unit 2
A 2 The man's got 3 The woman's got
  4 The man's got 5 The man's got
  6 've got

B 2 Have they got 3 Has he got
  4 Have they got 5 Have you got
  6 Has she got

C 2 Has the USA got a president? Yes, it has.
  3 Has Japan got a blue flag? No, it hasn't.
  4 Have Russia and the USA got a king?
    No, they haven't.
  5 Have the USA and India got a president?
    Yes, they have.
  6 Has Japan got a red and white flag?
    Yes, it has.

D 2 hasn't got 3 has got 4 haven't got
  5 has got 6 have got

E Answers will vary.
  1 has got / hasn't got
  2 has got / hasn't got
  3 has got / hasn't got
  4 've got / haven't got
  5 've got / haven't got

Unit 3
A 2 these 3 this 4 That 5 this 6 these

B 2 this 3 those 4 this 5 That 6 These

Unit 4
A 2 There are 3 there are 4 there is
  5 there is 6 there is

B 2 Are there two restaurants?
    No, there aren't.
  3 Is there a café? No, there isn't.
  4 Is there a car park? Yes, there is.
  5 Are there meeting rooms? Yes, there are.
  6 Is there a gym? Yes, there is.

Unit 5
A 2 Don't drink the water. 3 Be careful.
  4 Stop. 5 Don't turn left. 6 Don't eat this.

B 3 Walk 4 turn 5 Go 6 cross 7 Pass
  8 Take 9 turn 10 cross

Unit 6
A 2 her 3 his 4 theirs 5 hers 6 his 7 their

B 2 our 3 my 4 mine 5 ours 6 yours
  7 your

Unit 7
A 2 can't read Arabic very well
  3 can speak Arabic very well
  4 can understand Arabic very well
  5 can write Arabic quite well
  6 can't read Arabic at all

B 2 Can you read Russian?
  3 Can you speak Japanese?
  4 Can you understand English?
  5 Can you speak Spanish?
  6 Can you understand Arabic?

Unit 8

A 2 Paul's 3 women's 4 Smith's
   5 parents' 6 yesterday's 7 boss's
   8 babies' 9 nurse's
B 2 today's prices
   3 the make of the car
   4 your wife's driving licence
   5 the corner of the street
   6 car keys
   7 the front of the car
C Answers will vary.
   2 My father's first name is …
   3 My mother's favourite food is …
   4 My best friend's favourite sport is …
   5 My country's most famous writer is …
   6 My doctor's name is …

Unit 9

A 2 information 3 suggestions 4 advice
   5 work 6 dollars
B 2 any 3 piece of 4 any 5 some 6 a

Unit 10

A 2 me 3 them 4 him 5 her 6 he 7 they
   8 us
B 2 Put it in the bag.
   3 We'll telephone you tomorrow.
   4 You'll see them soon.
   5 Don't speak to her.
   6 Leave me your car.
   7 Don't come with them.
C 2 He … her 3 They … them
   4 She … him 5 She … him 6 He … him
   7 He … it
D Answers will vary.

Test 1 (Units 1–10)

A 1 Have 2 These 3 Is there 4 are there
   5 yours 6 its 7 well 8 Is there
B 1 Are 2 is 3 Are 4 aren't ('re not)
   5 Am 6 aren't ('re not)
C 1 I haven't got any sisters.
   2 Has Russia got a president?
   3 The USA hasn't got a king.
   4 We haven't got any money.
   5 Have they got the tickets?
D 1 Drive 2 Be 3 Stop 4 Don't stop
   5 Don't drive

E 1 our 2 me 3 mine 4 us 5 yours 6 his
F 1 my parent's house
   2 my mother's coat
   3 the capital of Germany
   4 today's newspaper
   5 the children's room
G 1 can't speak 2 Can … read
   3 can understand 4 Can … write
   5 can't hear
H 1 any 2 some 3 a 4 some 5 any
I 1 My sister is 2 I have 3 can't use
   4 some luggage 5 some advice

Unit 11

A 2 It's beginning. 3 They're swimming.
   4 We're moving. 5 You aren't going.
   6 She isn't stopping.
B 2 's drinking 3 isn't reading 4 is speaking
   5 isn't wearing 6 's eating 7 're sitting
   8 aren't working
C Answers will vary.
   1 I'm listening to / I'm not listening to
      music.
   2 I'm working / I'm not working in an
      office.
   3 I'm wearing / I'm not wearing jeans.
   4 I'm drinking / I'm not drinking coffee.
   5 I'm sitting / I'm not sitting on a train.

Unit 12

A 2 at 3 at 4 on 5 in 6 to
B 2 next to 3 behind 4 in front of 5 near
   6 opposite 7 between

Unit 13

A 3 No, she isn't.
   4 Yes, he is.
   5 She's working in Lisbon.
   6 She's visiting a client.
   7 Mark is meeting the Director.
   8 No, they aren't.
B 2 Is the sun shining in Lisbon?
   3 Are you enjoying life in London?
   4 What are you doing, Kirsty?
   5 Why is Mark meeting the Director?
   6 Who is attending the sales conference?
   7 Are you speaking on a mobile phone?

Unit 14

A 2 enjoys ... doesn't enjoy ... don't enjoy
   3 goes ... go ... don't go
   4 uses ... doesn't use ... use
   5 doesn't have ... have ... don't have
   6 does ... doesn't do ... don't do
   7 doesn't work ... work ... don't work
   8 likes ... doesn't like ... don't like

B 2 She usually reads
   3 I never understand
   4 We like
   5 We never stay
   6 My sister always works

C 2 need 3 work 4 leave 5 don't come
   6 has 7 think 8 get 9 don't know 10 isn't
   11 always attends

D 3 goes 4 swims 5 does 6 is working
   7 is staying 8 uses 9 listens
   10 doesn't sleep

Unit 15

A 2 ✗ 3 ✓ 4 ✗ 5 ✓ 6 ✗

B 2 sound wonderful 3 taste delicious
   4 look young 5 feel cold

C 2 Listen to this small new CD-player.
   3 Come to this big Italian restaurant.
   4 Try this new pink lipstick.
   5 We have modern American sportswear.

Unit 16

A 2 Do ... 3 Do ... 4 Do ... 5 Does ...
   6 Do ... 7 Does ... 8 Do ...

B Answers will vary.

C 2 Yes, I do. / No, I don't.
   3 Yes, I do. / No, I don't.
   4 Yes, I do. / No, I don't.
   5 Yes, he/she does. /No, he/she doesn't.
   6 Yes, they do. / No, they don't.
   7 Yes, he/she does. /No, he/she doesn't.
   8 Yes, I do. / No, I don't.

D 2 do you manage 3 do you sell
   4 do you drive 5 Do you travel
   6 does ... think 7 do ... give
   8 do you earn

E 2 manages 3 drives 4 sells
   5 doesn't travel 6 travels 7 give 8 earns

Unit 17

A 2 What 3 Why 4 How old 5 Where
   6 How much

B 2 When do people send Valentine cards?
   3 What is Cupid carrying in the picture?
   4 Who is Venus?
   5 How do we say 'zero' in tennis?
   6 Where is the Taj Mahal?
   2 b 3 a 4 d 5 e 6 c

Unit 18

A 2 He watches TV three times a week.
   3 He sometimes buys clothes.
   4 He goes on holiday once a year.
   5 He never eats in restaurants.
   6 He often rents videos.

B Answers will vary.

Unit 19

A 2 well 3 quietly 4 carefully 5 easily
   6 confidently 7 clearly 8 late
   9 neatly 10 hard 11 early 12 badly

B 2 late 3 neatly 4 confidently 5 clearly
   6 carefully 7 quickly

C Answers will vary.

Unit 20

A 2 were 3 were 4 was 5 were 6 was

B 2 How many ... were 3 Were
   4 Where was 5 Where were
   6 What ... was

C 2 There weren't ... There were
   3 There weren't ... There were
   4 wasn't ... was
   5 weren't ... were
   6 wasn't ... was

D 2 was/wasn't
   3 was/wasn't
   4 were/weren't
   5 was/wasn't
   6 were/weren't

Test 2 (Units 11–20)

A 1 's watching 2 are you 3 in
4 doesn't 5 wants 6 does he live
7 are there 8 go to work every day
9 good driver 10 fast

B 1 is swimming 2 Is it raining
3 is she meeting 4 are you doing
5 aren't leaving

C 1 teaches 2 doesn't like 3 do you have
4 does she start 5 don't speak

D 1 in 2 at 3 on 4 at 5 to

E 1 are you working
2 do you usually work
3 's raining
4 Are you having
5 often works

F 1 How old 2 Where 3 How much
4 Why 5 What

G 1 He doesn't always get up early.
2 Sue's got a beautiful coat.
3 He goes to the cinema twice a week.
4 He's got a big, red car.
5 She always works hard at the office.

H 1 wasn't 2 were 3 were 4 Was 5 Were

I 1 are they 2 in front of 3 next to 4 goes
5 nervous

Unit 21

A went, didn't finish,
didn't take, worked, met, was, left,
travelled, didn't have, took, had, got,
worked, became, stayed, sent, started,
bought, didn't stay, left, studied,

B 2 started /didn't start
3 grew up / didn't grow up
4 went / didn't go
5 took / didn't take
6 left / didn't leave
7 stayed / didn't stay
8 met / didn't meet
9 got / didn't get
10 had / didn't have
11 became / didn't become
12 sent / didn't send
13 bought / didn't buy
14 studied / didn't study
15 finished / didn't finish

C 3 left 4 didn't go 5 took
6 studied 7 didn't study 8 travelled
9 worked

D Answers will vary.

Unit 22

A 2 ✗ 3 the 4 the 5 ✗ 6 ✗ 7 the
a ✗ b the c ✗ ... ✗ d ✗ e ✗ f the g ✗
2 e 3 a 4 b 5 d 6 g 7 f

B 2 The ... the ... ✗
3 the
4 a ... the
5 The ... the ... the ... ✗
6 A ... a ... ✗

Unit 23

A 2 did you eat?
3 did they cost?
4 did she go?
5 did you meet?
6 did they leave?
7 did you buy?

B 2 When did ... walk
3 When did ... become
4 When did ... die
5 When did ... leave
6 When did ... win
7 When did ... start

C a In b On d In e In f On g On
a 3 b 2 d 7 e 6 f 5 g 4

D Answers will vary.

Unit 24

A 2 (a) He's going to be sick.
3 (f) You're going to have an accident.
4 (d) It isn't going to rain.
5 (c) We aren't going to arrive in time.
6 (g) I'm going to open the window.
7 (e) I'm going to stop the car!

B 2 What is he going to
3 Where are they going to
4 Who are you going to
5 Why is he going to
6 How much are you going to

C Answers will vary.
2 Yes, we are. / No, we aren't.
3 Yes, he/she is. / No, he/she isn't.
4 Yes, I am. / No, I'm not.
5 Yes, they are.
6 Yes, it is. / No, it isn't.

Unit 25

A 2 b 3 a 4 b 5 a 6 b

B 2 any 3 a 4 some 5 some 6 a 7 any
8 some

Unit 26

A 2 don't have to carry 3 don't have to vote
4 have to vote 5 have to stay
6 don't have to stay

B 2 have to wear 3 has to work
4 have to speak 5 has to drive
6 have to get up 7 has to look after

C 2 Does he have to work at night?
3 Do people in his job have to wear a suit?
4 Does he have to wear a uniform?
5 Do people in his job have to speak English?
6 Does he have to work long hours?
7 Do people in his job have to keep fit?
Pavel is an international pilot.

D Answers will vary.
1 Yes, I do. / No, I don't.
2 Yes, they do. / No, they don't.
3 Yes, they do. / No, they don't.
4 Yes, they do. / No, they don't.
5 Yes, I do. / No, I don't.
6 Yes, he or she does. / No, he or she doesn't.

Unit 27

A 2 taking 3 walk 4 cycle 5 catching 6 get
7 stay

B 2 seeing ... go 3 see ... going
4 get ... go 5 get ... give

Unit 28

A 3 doesn't eat any 4 doesn't eat much
5 doesn't eat many 6 doesn't eat any
7 eats a lot of 8 doesn't eat any

B Answers will vary.

C 2 How many glasses of water do you drink?
3 How much cheese do you eat?
4 How many eggs do you eat?
5 How many tomatoes do you eat?
6 How much milk do you drink?

Unit 29

A 2 more important 3 easier 4 more difficult
5 younger 6 more expensive 7 taller
8 faster 9 heavier 10 bigger
11 more modern 12 better

B 2 better 3 faster 4 more modern
5 more difficult 6 happier

C Suggested answers:
2 The Penton is heavier than the Canax.
3 The Penton is more expensive than the Canax.
4 The Canax is smaller than the Penton.
5 The Penton is better than the Canax.

Unit 30

A 2 the shortest 3 the fastest
4 the most interesting 5 the most expensive
6 the heaviest 7 the longest 8 the biggest
9 the most dangerous

B 2 shortest 3 biggest 4 most expensive
5 longest 6 fastest

C Answers will vary.

Test 3 (Units 21–30)

A 1 did he 2 last night 3 in 4 are you
5 don't have to 6 go 7 How many
8 getting 9 faster 10 heavier

B 1 the 2 ✗ 3 the 4 the 5 ✗

C 1 Where are you going to eat later?
2 Is she going to play tennis?
3 Does he have to get up early every day?
4 What exams do you have to take?
5 Are you going to be a teacher?

D 1 got 2 had 3 left 4 saw 5 bought

E 1 worked 2 didn't see 3 did you go
4 's going to rain 5 'm going to be

F 1 at 2 in 3 ago 4 yesterday 5 on

G 1 much 2 many 3 a lot of 4 much
5 many

H 1 younger than 2 the oldest
3 more expensive than
4 the most expensive 5 the hottest

I 1 the United States 2 the picture
3 going to watch 4 doesn't have to 5 open

Unit 31

A 2 listening 3 to speak
   4 to watch 5 waiting
B 2 to visit 3 to come 4 driving/to drive
   5 to come 6 to go 7 walking/to walk
   8 looking/to look 9 to see
C Answers will vary.

Unit 32

A 2 He's travelled to Brazil.
   3 They've travelled to Kenya.
   4 She's travelled to Russia.
   5 They haven't travelled to Singapore.
   6 She hasn't travelled to Poland.
B 2 've watched 3 've studied 4 've visited
   5 've never stayed 6 've never lived
C Answers will vary.
   2 've lived/haven't lived
   3 've travelled/haven't travelled
   4 've invited/haven't invited
   5 've tried/haven't tried
   6 've visited/haven't visited

Unit 33

A 2 given 3 eaten 4 seen 5 met 6 had
   7 taken 8 made 9 been 10 done
B 2 've just been 3 's just eaten
   4 've just given 5 's just taken
   6 've just had
C 2 Andy and Yama haven't met the Exton
   sales people yet.
   3 Mahmoud has given the new CD-ROMs
   to Kate.
   4 Yoriko hasn't seen the Sales Manager yet.
   5 Yama has made a new list of customers.
   6 Dan hasn't taken the new designs to the
   Tokyo office yet
D Answers will vary.

Unit 34

A 2 It's snowing. 3 It's 2 o'clock.
   4 It's 11 July. 5 It's 47 km to Glasgow.
   6 It's windy.
B 2 It's sunny 3 It's C 1°/It's cold
   4 It's windy 5 It's 19 6 It's 7
C Answers will vary.

Unit 35

A 2 Have you ever been to Australia?
   Yes, I have. / No, I haven't.
   3 Have you studied finance?
   Yes, I have. / No, I haven't.
   4 Have you taken exams in
   Accountancy?
   Yes, I have. / No, I haven't.
   5 Have you had a job in a big company?
   Yes, I have. / No, I haven't.
   6 Have you ever worked with a lot of
   people? Yes, I have. / No, I haven't.
B 2 Have I missed the train for Hull?
   No, you haven't.
   3 Has the train for Perth already left?
   No, it hasn't.
   4 Have we missed the train for Stoke?
   Yes, you have.
   5 Have the Stoke and York trains left yet?
   Yes, they have.
   6 Have I missed the train for Perth?
   No, you haven't.

Unit 36

A 2 Can you send my son this letter?
   3 She showed us the postcard.
   4 Can you send me the bill?
   5 Please buy me a pen.
   6 He cooked her a meal.
B 2 Mark a video. 3 his mother a watch.
   4 Karen a guitar. 5 Jane some chocolates.
   6 Karen a mobile phone. 7 Mark a camera.
C 2 Can you buy her a drink?
   3 I lent him some money.
   4 Please read me this letter.
   (Read me this letter, please.)
   5 I cooked her a great meal.
   6 Can you pass me the salt?

Unit 37

A 2 were sitting 3 were doing 4 was waiting
   5 was wearing 6 was carrying
B 2 were watching 3 was having
   4 was working 5 wasn't staying
   6 weren't feeling
C Answers will vary.

Unit 38

A 2 'm going to 3 will 4 are going to
   5 's going to 6 Will
B 2 I'm going to take 3 I won't be
   4 is he going to work 5 I'll close
   6 She'll tell 7 I'm not going to watch

Unit 39

A 2 He was playing football.
   3 No, they weren't.
   4 They were playing cards.
   5 No, she wasn't.
   6 Yes, she was.
B 2 were you living
   3 Were you studying
   4 was your best friend living
   5 Was it raining
   6 were you doing
   (Answers will vary.)

Unit 40

A 2 leave … 'm going to travel / 'll travel
   3 return … 'm going to work / 'll work
   4 finish … 'm going to find / 'll find
   5 'm going to apply / 'll apply … 'm
   6 get … 'm going to look / 'll look
B 2 If you pass … 'll do
   3 If you take … 'll study
   4 If you fail … 'll take
   5 'll do … you fail
   6 If you pass … 'll study
C Answers will vary.

Test 4 (Units 31–40)

A 1 going 2 It's 3 me 4 was she 5 it's
   6 reading 7 I went 8 me 9 to have
   10 is it
B 1 She has never lived in Greece.
   2 Have they already had dinner?
   3 Has our bus left yet?
   4 They haven't eaten lunch yet.
   5 I haven't lost it.
C 1 It was raining.
   2 She wasn't looking.
   3 Were they working?
   4 What was he doing?
   5 Who were they meeting?
D 1 to see 2 to have 3 getting up
   4 working 5 to go
E 1 'll 2 is going to 3 is he going to
   4 Will you 5 'm going to
F 1 go … 'm going to wear / 'll wear
   2 see … 'll tell
   3 was standing
   4 Have you had
   5 has already left
G 1 Have you ever eaten Thai food?
   2 I gave her a present.
   3 Did you write me a letter?
   4 Is it a long way?
   5 Where was she working last year?
H 1 want to have 2 is it 3 enjoy swimming
   4 is 5 get
I 1 eaten 2 cut 3 broken 4 given 5 lost

Acknowledgements

I am very grateful to the following teachers from all around the world who have commented on the material:

Jania Barrell, UK
Vera Dvorakova, Czech Republic
Thérèse Elliott, France
Cinzia Riguzzi, Italy
Peter Strutt, France
Olga Vinogradova, Russia
Lo Wei Yee, Singapore.

I would particularly like to thank Alison Sharpe for her help, guidance and support during the editing of this series. My thanks also to Anna Teevan for her expert editing of the material and to Jo Barker and Tony O'Connell for their excellent design and artwork.

The publisher would like to thank the following for permission to reproduce photographs.

Corbis: pages 16, 23, 27, 34, 38, 43, 60